Jenna S. Rogers

MW00947840

THIS BOOK BELONGS TO:

INTRODUCTION

Welcome to Your Self-Care Advent Calendar

Hello, Sister

We're going to go on a lovely and purposeful trip together, so welcome to your Self-Care Advent Calendar. This is a celebration of you, your health, and the amazing power of little, meaningful actions of self-care—not simply another countdown to the holidays. We'll talk about how to take care of your mind, body, and spirit over the course of the next 24 days, all while embracing the happiness and tranquility that come from prioritizing yourself.

It's simple to get sucked into the maelstrom of obligations, events, and expectations during the Christmas season. **We frequently discover that we give so much of our time, effort, and affection to other people while ignoring the most crucial relationship of all: the one we have with ourselves.** This calendar is an invitation for you to make that happen. It serves as a gentle reminder that you are worthy of time spent on yourself, reflecting, recharging, and finding your true priorities.

You'll find a mild prompt or action every day to help you live a bit more joyful, peaceful, and balanced. These aren't just chores to cross off a list; they're chances to take a moment to relax, take deep breaths, and treat yourself with the love and attention you so generously provide to others. These practices are all about honoring you, whether that means pausing to reflect on your path, enjoying a warm cup of tea, or just taking a moment to enjoy yourself.

And here is where this journey's charm lies: it's really intimate. There's no need to execute anything flawlessly, and there are no right or incorrect methods to approach it. On some days, you might throw yourself into the activity with all of your might, while on other days, you might require something more contemplative, subdued, or quiet. That's acceptable at all. The objective is to embrace the notion that self-care is a need rather than a luxury, to listen to your heart, and to become aware of what you need each day.

Making time for self-care is more than just giving yourself a little "me time." Your physical, emotional, and mental well-being are being actively supported. Regular self-care activities have been demonstrated to lessen stress, lessen anxiety, and enhance general wellbeing, which is supported by science. You can strengthen your immune system, elevate your mood, and even get better sleep by doing these things. By taking care of yourself, you not only nourish your body and mind but also build your resilience and ability to handle life's setbacks with positively and grace.

This journey of self-care is about more than just the next twenty-four hours; it's about setting the stage for a life that is more joyful, balanced, and attentive. It's about forming routines that will benefit you long after the holidays are over. It also involves realizing that you can better support the people and interests you love when you look after yourself.

You are not alone as we embark on this adventure together, so remember that. We're embracing the joy of self-care with open hearts as we travel this path together, supporting one another along the way. Let every day be an occasion to honor your fortitude, generosity, and dedication to yourself. This calendar should serve as a source of inspiration, solace, and happiness—a constant reminder that you are deserving of all the love and care in the world.

Sister, let's celebrate a month of self-care. Let's use these 24 days to contemplate, rejuvenate. Let's carry this energy into the upcoming year and beyond.

GRATITUDE JOURNALING

1
December

Hey Beautiful,

As we begin this journey of self-care together, I want to invite you to take a moment just for yourself—just for your heart. Today, let's start with something simple yet so powerful: gratitude.

Choose a comfortable place to sit, maybe with a nice cup of tea, a piece of paper, and your favorite notebook. Inhale deeply, close your eyes for a brief moment, and list **three aspects of your life that bring you joy.** It could be someone, an occasion, a tiny, lovely thing, or even a significant accomplishment that makes you feel proud.

List each one of them one by one. Sister, don't stop there. Think about why these things are important to you for a second. What makes you happy about them? What is it about them that makes life brighter for you? Making a list isn't the only thing to do here; you also need to embrace those emotions and allow them to surround you with love and optimism.

....

....

....

....

....

....

....

....

....

....

....

....

And here's something that may surprise you: **the effectiveness of this practice is supported by actual science.** Regular thankfulness practice has been linked to healthier relationships, greater mental health, and even a stronger immune system, according to studies. It can make you feel happier, less stressed, and change your perspective from what you lack to what you have plenty of in your life. You are, therefore, gently invigorating both your mind and body during this moment of self-care.

This little activity helps you anchor yourself in what really matters, especially as the days get busier and the outside world seems a bit more frenetic. **It's not simply about counting your blessings. You are deserving of this quiet time for introspection.** Recall that you have this area, this time, and your thanks. Allow it to fill you with warmth and know that I am walking this route beside you.

2 December

PAMPER YOURSELF

Hey Gorgeous,
After starting our journey with gratitude, it's time to take things up a notch and give yourself the gift of pure relaxation—you deserve it! Today is all about pampering yourself, so let's create a spa day right in the comfort of your own home. Think of it as a love letter to your body, mind, and soul.

Whether it's in the morning, midday, or evening, set aside some time today. Make the most of this moment; it's yours. **First, set the ideal mood** by lighting candles, diffusing your favorite essential oils, and turning on calming music that relaxes you. Allow the world beyond your door to disappear.

Let's start the pampering now. Perhaps you'll treat yourself to a rich face mask that makes your skin glow, or you'll take a warm bath with bubbles, bath salts, or even petals from flowers—whatever it is that makes you feel like the goddess that you are. Let your problems melt into the water as you soak. Alternatively, you may go all out and devote time to enjoying every step of a comprehensive skincare routine, which includes exfoliation and moisturizing. Keep in mind that it's not just about your skin; it's also about how every touch, smell, and caring moment makes you feel.

Treating oneself is a strong act of self-love and care, not merely a luxury. You can use it to persuade yourself, "I am worthy of this kindness, this time, and this effort." And what do you know? Science supports the significance of this. **It has been demonstrated that self-care activities like skincare and relaxation lower stress levels, elevate mood, and even enhance quality of sleep.** By taking care of your skin, you're strengthening your relationship with yourself, improving your emotional health, and enhancing your confidence.

Give yourself permission to really relax today. Allow yourself to be reminded of how valuable you are by the soothing warmth of the bath, the cooling sensation of the mask, and the delicate regimen of your skincare routines. **You are taking care of your spirit and filling your cup to allow you to shine even more brightly than just your physical needs.**

And never forget that you are not doing this by yourself. In spirit, I'm right here with you, enjoying the positive energy and commemorating this lovely instance of self-love. **Without any hesitation or shame, take this time for yourself because you are valuable and worthy of every moment.**

DIGITAL DETOX

3 December

Hey Sister,
Today, we're taking a bold step into something that might feel a little challenging but is so important for our well-being—a digital detox. Yep, that's right! It's time to unplug from social media, step away from unnecessary screen time, and give ourselves the gift of being fully present in the moment. Trust me, this is going to feel like a breath of fresh air.

Our phones, laptops, and TVs are always around us, and although they keep us engaged and connected, they may also drain us without our knowledge. The urge to always be "on," never-ending scrolling, and incessant notifications can make us feel overwhelmed and cut off from what really matters. **Let's allow ourselves to take a step back today, even if it's only for a single day.**

Turn off your phone's notifications, set it to "Do Not Disturb," or even place it in a different room to start your day. Try to restrict your screen time while working to what is absolutely essential. Avoid social media completely, including scrolling and checking in, if at all possible. Instead, use this time to reestablish your connection to the outside world. Perhaps the beauty of the early light coming through your window or the sound of the birds outdoors will catch your attention. Maybe when you're talking to your loved ones, you'll find that you're more in the moment, paying attention and participating without the distraction of a screen.

The incredible thing is that research confirms the potential benefits of this. **Research has indicated that taking a vacation from electronic gadgets can help us sleep better, feel less stressed, and experience less anxiety.** By disengaging from the ceaseless barrage of data and comparison that accompanies social media, we allow our minds to recuperate and rejuvenate. We may sharpen our concentration, increase our inventiveness, and rediscover the delight of everyday situations. Additionally, when we learn to be more aware of and present for those around us, it can improve our relationships.

Make an effort to spend as much time as possible on soul-nourishing activities while on your digital detox. Perhaps take a walk in the outdoors, read a book you've been meaning to get around to, or just spend some quality time with the people you care about. No screens, just genuine interaction. Maybe even take up a new pastime or just relax and enjoy a day without using any screens.

This is about allowing oneself space to breathe, think, and just be, not about isolating yourself from the outside world forever. You may feel lighter, more in control, and closer to what matters most at the end of the day. Who knows? You may even be motivated to incorporate digital detoxification into your self-care regimen on a regular basis.

4
December

MINDFUL BREATHING

Hey Lovely,

Today, we're going to slow things down and focus on something simple yet incredibly powerful—our breath. It's easy to overlook in our busy lives, but your breath is a constant companion, always with you, and it holds an incredible power to calm, center, and heal. So today, let's take 10 minutes just for ourselves to practice mindful breathing—something that's small but can make such a big difference in how we feel.

Look for a peaceful area where you can comfortably sit or lie down. Simply begin by closing your eyes, letting your shoulders drop, and inhaling deeply through your nose. As you fill it with oxygen, feel your belly grow. After holding the breath for a short while, release any tension or stress you may be carrying by softly releasing it through your mouth. **As you exhale, feel your body release tension.** Maintain this rhythm, paying attention to each breath in and out, and let the constant rise and fall of your breath to lull you into a state of tranquility.

As you go, you could find that your thoughts are starting to stray. Perhaps they are returning to your to-do list or the conversation you had the day before. It's alright! Simply return your attention to your breathing. **The beauty of mindful breathing lies in the fact that it doesn't need perfection or flawless mental clarity.** Instead, it simply requires you to be in the moment, accept any ideas or emotions that come up, and then allow them to pass as you return to the constant, peaceful flow of your breath.

The goal of mindful breathing is self-reconnection, not only relaxation. Often times, when life seems chaotic and our minds are racing, we forget to take a deep breath. We grow breathless due to the maelstrom of tasks, which only makes us more stressed. **The good news is that research indicates that even a brief period of time spent engaging in deep, focused breathing exercises can lower blood pressure, lessen anxiety, and even enhance concentration.** It can relax your nervous system and give you a more centered, grounded feeling. It can also strengthen your immune system, enhance digestion, and help you sleep better. Who knew that something as basic as breathing could have such a significant impact on our health and happiness?

Thus, give the gift of careful breathing to yourself today. Breathe in fully, relish the calm that comes with each release of breath, and claim this moment as your own. **You're feeding not just your body but also your mind and soul by reminding yourself that you can always come back to this peaceful location, no matter what's going on in the world.**

MINDFUL BREATHING EXERCISE

Heart-Centered Breathing for Calm and Confidence

This exercise will help you reconnect with your inner strength and calm by focusing on the heart area.

Instructions:

1. Sit in a comfortable position, either on a chair or cross-legged on the floor. Keep your back straight but relaxed.
2. Close your eyes and place one hand on your heart.
3. Take a deep breath in through your nose, slowly counting to 4 as you imagine your breath moving directly into your heart.
4. Hold the breath for a count of 2, feeling the warmth of your hand on your chest.
5. Exhale slowly through your mouth for a count of 6, imagining any stress or tension melting away from your heart.
6. Repeat this cycle 5-10 times, focusing on feelings of calm and confidence growing with each breath.
7. After the last exhale, pause for a moment before opening your eyes and gently returning to your day.

Benefit: This exercise helps to cultivate self-compassion and calm, particularly beneficial during moments of anxiety or self-doubt.

5
December

AROMATHERAPY

Hey Beautiful,
Today, we're going to dive into something truly soothing—aromatherapy. It's time to fill your space with calming scents and let the power of fragrance work its magic on your mind and body. Trust me, this is one of those little things that can make a big difference in how you feel, especially as we journey together through this season of self-care.

The main goal of aromatherapy is to create a peaceful, relaxing, and well-being-promoting environment with scented candles or essential oils. **It's an easy yet effective technique to lift your spirits, declutter, and find your inner self again.** Therefore, now is the ideal time to surround yourself with aromas that uplift you, whether you're relaxing after a hard day or just need a little pick-me-up.

Select a smell that makes you feel good to start. There are tons of possibilities, and each has special advantages of its own. A tried-and-true remedy for relaxation, lavender helps release tension and stress and is ideal for using right before bed. When you're feeling a little congested or overwhelmed, eucalyptus is wonderful for clearing your head and making breathing easier. Orange and lemon smells, in particular, are stimulating and upbeat, making them ideal for elevating your spirits and adding a little sunshine to your day. Alternatively, perhaps you're drawn to the earthiness of sandalwood or the warmth of vanilla, both of which contribute to a cosy, comfortable ambiance.

It's time to furnish your haven after selecting your fragrance. You can diffuse essential oils, light fragrant candles, or even add a few drops to your bath. You can just add a few drops of essential oil to a bowl of hot water and let the steam spread the aroma throughout the room if you don't have a diffuser. Take a moment to close your eyes and inhale deeply as the aroma fills the room. **Allow the aroma to comfort and melt away your stress, enveloping you like a loving hug.**

The wonderful part is that aromatherapy is more than just a way to enjoy pleasant scents. There's actual science to it! **Studies have demonstrated that specific smells can cause the brain to release feel-good chemicals like dopamine and serotonin, which can alleviate anxiety, elevate mood, and even encourage sounder sleep.** The limbic system, which governs emotions and memories, is another area of the brain that essential oils can interact with to promote feelings of peace and wellbeing. Therefore, aromatherapy is not merely a form of self-indulgence; it also serves to promote mental and emotional well-being.

Including aromatherapy in your self-care arsenal can be quite beneficial. It serves as a reminder that caring for oneself doesn't always need to be a huge deal; sometimes, the little things that add up to a big picture are the most meaningful. Your body and mind will be able to unwind, reset, and regenerate as you inhale these calming aromas.

Thus, use this opportunity to immerse yourself completely in the experience now. Perhaps you'll combine your aromatherapy with a soothing yoga session, a quiet time with a nice book, or a relaxing bath. **Allow the aroma to take you away to a serene location and serve as a gentle reminder that you deserve this time to yourself.**

6
December

NATURE WALK

Hey Sister,
Today, we're stepping outside to reconnect with the world around us. It's time for a peaceful walk in nature—a chance to breathe in the fresh air, soak in the beauty of the outdoors, and let the natural world work its calming magic on your soul. Trust me, this is exactly what we need to feel grounded and refreshed.

Give yourself a moment to put any concerns or distractions behind you as you leave. You should use this walk to unwind, rejuvenate, and just be in the now. **Allow yourself to lose yourself in the moment, whether you're hiking nearby, strolling through a park, or strolling by the lake.**

Start by concentrating on the surrounding sights. Take note of the leaves' many hues, the way the sun streams through the trees, and the exquisite designs on the flowers and other plants. Allow your gaze to stray and notice the little things that, in our hectic lives, we frequently miss. Listen to the sounds of nature after that. Perhaps it's the sound of birds chirping, leaves rustling in the breeze, or the soft run of a nearby stream. Allow these noises to anchor you in the here and now and help you to become more aware of the present.

Remember to enjoy the scents as well. Allow your senses to be filled with these organic scents, whether it's the sharpness of the air, the freshness of the grass, or the earthy perfume of the soil. **Nature has a way of awakening all our senses and serving as a constant reminder of the small pleasures in life.**

Being in nature has a very specific effect on us; it's like hitting the reset button for our bodies and thoughts. And what do you know? Science concurs! **Spending time in nature has been linked to lowered blood pressure, improved mood, and reduced stress, according to studies. It can also strengthen your defenses against illness, spark your creativity, and make you feel more a part of the world.** Shinrin-yoku, or "forest bathing," is the phrase used by the Japanese to describe this practice, which entails immersing oneself in the natural world and enjoying its numerous health advantages.

Try not to think about the next thing on your to-do list as you stroll. Rather, pay attention to your breathing, the cadence of your movements, and the beauty all around you. **Let this be a moving meditation, where you get closer to a state of clarity and calmness with each step.**

7

December

HYDRATION REMINDER

Hey Lovely,
Today, we're focusing on something simple but absolutely essential—hydration. I know it's easy to forget to drink enough water, especially when life gets busy, but today is all about making a conscious effort to give your body the hydration it needs. Trust me, your body and mind will thank you for it!

Get a large glass of water first thing in the morning, before you have coffee or anything else. This short routine can remind you to keep sipping as the hours pass and can set the tone for the remainder of the day. Would it not be more fun if you added a cool twist? For a taste explosion, add some cucumber, lemon, or even a few berries. Try adding fresh herbs, such as basil or mint, if you're feeling really fancy. Whatever gets you thrilled to drink up!

Keep that water bottle by your side and remember to take frequent sips as you go about your day. Use an app that tracks your intake or set simple reminders on your phone if you have trouble remembering things. Not only should you drink more water, but you should also really notice how it makes you feel—better overall, more energised, and focused.

You know, there's a lot more to staying hydrated than just slake your thirst. Nearly every bodily function depends on water. It promotes healthy digestion, maintains skin radiance, helps control body temperature, and even benefits the brain. You're more likely to feel alert, less worn out, and happier when you're properly hydrated. Not to mention, staying properly hydrated will help reduce headaches and increase the effectiveness of your workouts.

Hydration is also supported by some very amazing research. **Even slight dehydration can have an impact on your mood and ability to concentrate, according to studies.** All you have to do is make sure your brain gets enough water to keep it running smoothly. Drinking enough water also keeps your joints lubricated, aids in the removal of toxins from your body, and guarantees that your organs are operating at peak performance.

So let's focus on staying hydrated today. Consider it a simple, practical, and very helpful self-care practice. To add even more special touches, give yourself a cute water bottle or infuser that brings you joy each time you reach for it.

One drink at a time, we're tending to our bodies and minds, and it feels wonderful to take care of ourselves in this way. **Let's continue to glow from the inside out while you continue to sip and feel rejuvenated.**

8 December

INDULGE IN A GOOD BOOK

Hey Sister,
Today, we're diving into one of life's simplest yet most profound pleasures—getting lost in a good book. Whether you're a lifelong book lover or someone who's been meaning to make more time for reading, today is the perfect day to slow down, curl up, and let yourself be carried away by the pages of a story that inspires you, relaxes you, or maybe even takes you on a little adventure.

Consider the genre of book you are now reading. Perhaps the novel will enthrall you with its romance or mystery. Alternatively, it might be a self-help book that provides guidance and inspiration to help you develop and think. Poetry, in which each word seems to have a tiny piece of enchantment, or memoirs that provide a glimpse into the life and experiences of another person may pique your interest. **Whatever it is, take up a book that seems to be the ideal partner for this moment—one that speaks to you personally today.**

Now, locate your most comfortable place. It could be a corner of your preferred café, your bed piled high with pillows, or a cozy chair by the window. Take a blanket, brew a hot cup of tea or coffee, and take a moment to step back and observe the outside world. This is your moment, your getaway, your opportunity to engage with the concepts and language that ease your spirit or spark your imagination.

Reading is a wonderful method to take care of yourself because it feeds your mind and spirit in addition to providing amusement. By reading, you grant yourself permission to escape the chaos and clamor of daily life and enter a realm of possibility. Reading has a special way of broadening your views and instilling a sense of peace and clarity, whether you're learning about a new subject, getting insight into the viewpoint of another person, or coming up with fresh ideas for your own life.

Not to mention the science involved! **It has been demonstrated that reading greatly reduces stress; reading for just six minutes can reduce stress by more than two thirds. Additionally, it enhances brain activity, maintaining mental clarity and interest.** Several brain regions are activated when you lose yourself in a story, which improves your vocabulary, empathy, and creative thinking. Moreover, reading before bed can enhance your quality of sleep by assisting with relaxation and the shift to a more restful sleep cycle.

Go ahead and start reading that book you've been eyeing or pick up an old favorite today. **Give yourself permission to lose yourself in the story's narrative flow, rhythm, and internalized feelings.** There's no rush, so take your time. Give yourself permission to savor every moment of reading, regardless of how long it takes.

A LIST OF INTERESTING BOOKS:

For Romance Lovers:
- "The Seven Husbands of Evelyn Hugo" by Taylor Jenkins Reid
- A glamorous, emotionally charged novel that dives into Hollywood's golden age, filled with romance, secrets, and love stories that transcend time.

For Mystery Enthusiasts:
- "The Silent Patient" by Alex Michaelides
- A psychological thriller that will keep you guessing with its twists and turns. Perfect for those who love unraveling puzzles.

For Self-Help & Growth:

- "Atomic Habits" by James Clear
- A guide to transforming your life through small changes. Clear's actionable advice will inspire and help you build better habits.

For Poetry Admirers:

- "The Sun and Her Flowers" by Rupi Kaur
- A collection of poems that explores growth, healing, and self-love, perfect for a moment of reflection and inner peace.

For Memoir Readers:

- "Becoming" by Michelle Obama
- A deeply personal memoir by the former First Lady, chronicling her journey from the South Side of Chicago to the White House, offering inspiration and insight.

For Historical Fiction Fans:

- "The Nightingale" by Kristin Hannah
- A moving story about two sisters in France during World War II, exploring their courage, resilience, and survival in a time of war.

For Fantasy Escapists:

- "The House in the Cerulean Sea" by TJ Klune
- A heartwarming and enchanting tale of magical children and an unexpected family, perfect for those seeking comfort and a touch of whimsy.

For Classic Novel Lovers:

- "Pride and Prejudice" by Jane Austen
- A timeless romance with wit, humor, and the complexities of social class, love, and family, set in Regency-era England..

For Adventure Seekers:

- "The Alchemist" by Paulo Coelho
- A philosophical journey of a young shepherd who follows his dreams, exploring themes of destiny, personal growth, and the pursuit of happiness.

9 December

AFFIRMATIONS

Hey Beautiful,

Today, we're focusing on something truly powerful—affirmations. It's time to tap into the strength of your own words, to uplift yourself with positive, empowering statements that resonate deeply with your soul. Affirmations are like little seeds of positivity that, when nurtured, can grow into a strong, unshakable mindset. So let's take this day to plant those seeds together and watch them bloom.

Start by setting out some time for yourself in a quiet place where you feel comfortable and at ease. Shut your eyes, take a deep breath, and ask yourself, "**What do I need to hear today?**" What are the phrases that will give me confidence, support, and a sense of worth? It's possible that you've been experiencing some overwhelm and may use the reassurance that "I am enough, just as I am." Or maybe you're working toward a significant objective and you need to tell yourself, "I can achieve my goals." Perhaps it's something as straightforward yet deep as "I trust myself and my journey," or "I deserve love and happiness." Let these affirmations be genuine, heartfelt, and specific to your needs, whatever they may be.

Once your affirmations are selected, put them in writing. **To keep these uplifting words close at hand throughout the day, you can scribble them in your diary, put them on sticky notes to post about your house, or even set them as phone reminders.** After that, spend some time speaking them aloud while allowing each phrase to sink in. Sometimes we need to be our own best friends, therefore speak with conviction and as though you're sharing these realities with a close buddy.

Throughout the day, remember these affirmations. Recite them whenever you see doubt beginning to creep in, when you need a confidence boost, or even just to reaffirm your positive feelings while you're feeling wonderful. **The more times you hear them, the more they become ingrained in your mind, influencing your thoughts and emotions.**

And here's the thing: there is actual research behind the effectiveness of affirmations; they are not just feel-good platitudes. **You are practically rewiring your brain when you repeat positive affirmations on a regular basis.** Because of a property of our brains known as neuroplasticity, our minds may adjust and change in response to the ideas and experiences we have. You may teach your brain to concentrate on the positive, develop a more upbeat mindset, and increase your self-confidence by concentrating on positive affirmations.

Affirmations can lower stress, increase self-esteem, and even enhance your capacity for problem-solving under duress, according to research. They function by stimulating the brain's reward regions, which contributes to an increase in optimism and fortitude. As a result, when you repeat these affirmations, you're actually bringing about significant, constructive change in both your body and mind.

Because affirmations give you the ability to take charge of your inner dialogue, they are an incredibly effective kind of self-care. Thoughts of doubt, fear, or negativity are common, but you may choose to replace them with positive thoughts and self-love by using affirmations. It's similar to giving yourself a brief pep talk to remind you of how wonderful you really are.

So, today, give your voice some strength. May you find solace, support, and strength in these affirmations. Talk to them lovingly and with confidence in your words. **Positive seeds that you sow will blossom into a garden of confidence and self-love.**

AFFIRMATIONS:

"I embrace the beauty of my unique journey, trusting that every step I take, even the small ones, leads me closer to my true purpose."

"As the year comes to a close, I release the expectations placed upon me by others and honor the woman I am becoming, unapologetically and authentically."

"I choose to fill my days with compassion and grace, knowing that my worth is not defined by external accomplishments but by the love and kindness I give and receive."

"During this season of reflection, I grant myself the gift of peace, allowing myself to rest without guilt, knowing that caring for my soul is essential."

"I trust in my ability to navigate the uncertainties of life, finding strength in my resilience and grace in my growth, no matter the challenges I face."

MY AFFIRMATIONS:

....

....

....

....

....

....

....

10
December

CREATIVE EXPRESSION

Hey Creative Soul,
Today is all about letting your imagination run free and expressing yourself through creativity. Whether you're a seasoned artist or someone who hasn't picked up a paintbrush in years, this is your day to dive into the joy of making something with your hands and heart. Let's embrace the power of creative expression together and see where it takes us!

Consider the types of creative endeavors that you find exciting. Perhaps it's writing poetry or creating art, crafts, or drawings. Maybe you've always wanted to give something new a shot, like knitting, jewelry-making, or taking pictures. You have today to investigate whatever it may be. **The freedom to follow your intuition and observe what happens when you express yourself creatively is what makes it so beautiful.**

Locate a cozy area where you may create your creative retreat. Whether it's paint and canvas, paper and pencils, or an assortment of craft items, gather your stuff. Play some upbeat music, or just take in the solitude, and lose yourself in the moment. This isn't about perfection, so don't worry about the result. It's about letting your inner artist come out, having fun on the trip, and experimenting with colors, forms, and ideas.

Because it enables you to establish a special and profound connection with yourself, creative expression is a potent kind of self-care. You are giving yourself permission to explore, to try new things, and to express feelings and ideas that may be difficult to articulate when you work on creative projects. It's a method to process what's inside of you, a way to let go, and it can be really healing.

And this is supported by some amazing science! **Research has demonstrated that being creative can lower stress and anxiety, boost happiness, and even enhance cognitive performance.** Dopamine is a "feel-good" chemical that your brain releases when you create, elevating your mood and giving you a sense of success. As you concentrate on the here and now and the creative process, mindfulness is also promoted by creative expression. This helps to calm the mind and lessen the cacophony of daily stress.

So go ahead and have fun today. Make something that is unique to you, something that brings a grin to your face, or something that enables you to communicate whatever is on your mind or in your heart. **Additionally, don't be afraid to get messy—occasionally, the most creative works result from unstructured, spontaneous situations.**

Recall that creativity is primarily about the process rather than the result. It's all about enjoying yourself, letting go, and learning something new about yourself in the process. Take advantage of this time to connect with your inner artist and explore and express yourself. Your artistic expression is a stunning representation of your incredible nature.

11 December

TREAT YOURSELF TO A HEALTHY MEAL

Hey Sister,
Today is all about nourishing yourself from the inside out by treating yourself to a healthy, delicious meal. Whether you love to cook or prefer to order in, today's focus is on enjoying something that makes your body feel good and your taste buds happy. Let's take this opportunity to slow down, savor the flavors, and give our bodies the love and care they deserve.

Why not make your favorite nutritious cuisine in the kitchen if you're feeling up to it? Perhaps it's a robust grain bowl with all your favorite toppings, a vibrant salad bursting with fresh vegetables, or a hot, soothing soup that lifts your spirits. **Whether you're chopping, stirring, or seasoning, cooking can be a meditative process. It all comes down to being in the moment and appreciating the simple act of making something nourishing for yourself.** It's also acceptable if cooking isn't your thing right now! It's also great to order something healthy from your favorite restaurant. The secret is to pick an activity that gives you a sense of fulfillment and energy.

After your dinner is prepared, pause to arrange the space. Maybe arrange the table elegantly, light a candle, or find a comfortable place to relax. **Take a few calm breaths, acknowledge your body's need for nourishment, and express some thanks for the meal in front of you before you start eating.** Savor every taste as you eat. Take note of the flavors, textures, and sensations the food evokes in you. A wonderful approach to establish a connection with your body, pay attention to its requirements, and enjoy the small joys of a satisfying meal is to eat thoughtfully.

Eating healthily is about taking better care of oneself on a deeper level than merely providing for your physical needs. By selecting nutrient-dense foods, you're providing your body with the resources it needs to flourish. Eating well-prepared meals can give you more energy, elevate your mood, and make you feel more balanced all around. Not to mention the long-term advantages, which include lowering the chance of developing chronic illnesses, preserving a healthy weight, and bolstering a robust immune system.

The practice of mindful eating is also supported by some amazing scientific findings. **Eating with awareness increases your ability to detect fullness, which aids in portion management and helps you avoid overindulging.** Better digestion has also been related to mindful eating, as your body can more effectively break down and absorb nutrients when you chew your food well and consume it slowly. Additionally, it can make eating a more pleasurable and deliberate experience, which can help you develop a healthier connection with food and reduce stress.

So treat yourself to a delicious lunch that will make you feel fantastic as well as taste amazing today. Enjoy every moment of this time, whether you're ordering your favorite healthy cuisine or cooking up a storm. You're fueling your spirit in addition to your body when you eat.

Roasted Winter Vegetable & Quinoa Salad

Ingredients :

For the Salad:

- 1 cup quinoa, rinsed
- 2 cups vegetable broth (or water)
- 2 medium carrots, peeled and chopped
- 1 medium sweet potato, peeled and chopped
- 1 small butternut squash, peeled, seeded, and chopped
- 1 red onion, chopped
- 1 tablespoon olive oil
- 1 teaspoon smoked paprika
- 1 teaspoon ground cumin
- Salt and pepper to taste
- 1/2 cup pomegranate seeds
- 1/4 cup chopped fresh parsley or cilantro
- 1/4 cup toasted pumpkin seeds or almonds (optional)

For the Citrus Dressing:

- 1/4 cup fresh orange juice
- 1 tablespoon lemon juice
- 1 tablespoon lime juice
- 2 tablespoons olive oil
- 1 tablespoon maple syrup or honey
- 1 teaspoon Dijon mustard
- Salt and pepper to taste
-

Steps :

1. *Cook the Quinoa:*
In a medium pot, bring the vegetable broth (or water) to a boil. Add the rinsed quinoa, reduce heat to low, cover, and simmer for 15 minutes, or until all the liquid is absorbed. Fluff with a fork and set aside.

2. *Roast the Vegetables:*
Preheat your oven to 400°F (200°C).
In a large bowl, toss the chopped carrots, sweet potato, butternut squash, and red onion with olive oil, smoked paprika, ground cumin, salt, and pepper.
Spread the vegetables evenly on a baking sheet and roast for 25-30 minutes, or until they are golden brown and tender. Stir halfway through for even roasting.

3. *Prepare the Dressing:*
In a small bowl, whisk together the orange juice, lemon juice, lime juice, olive oil, maple syrup (or honey), Dijon mustard, salt, and pepper. Taste and adjust seasoning as needed.

4. *Assemble the Salad:*
In a large salad bowl, combine the cooked quinoa and roasted vegetables. Add the pomegranate seeds, fresh parsley or cilantro, and toasted pumpkin seeds or almonds (if using).
Drizzle the citrus dressing over the salad and toss gently to combine.

5. *Serve:*
Serve the salad warm or at room temperature. This salad can be enjoyed as a light meal on its own or as a festive side dish for a December gathering.

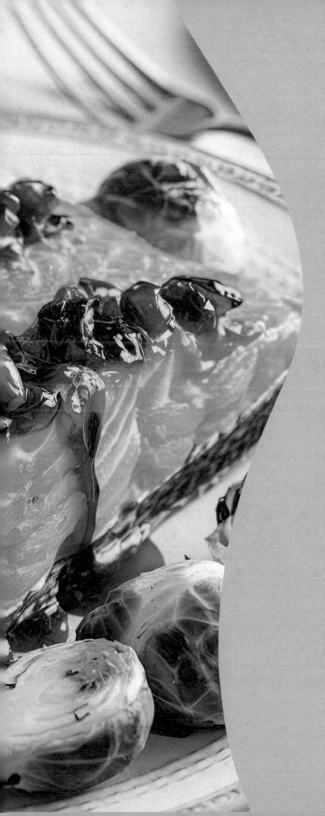

Baked Salmon with Cranberry-Orange Glaze

Ingredients :

Ingredients:

For the Salmon:

- 4 salmon fillets (about 6 oz each)
- Salt and pepper, to taste
- 1 tablespoon olive oil

For the Cranberry-Orange Glaze:

- 1/2 cup fresh cranberries (or frozen, thawed)
- 1/4 cup fresh orange juice
- Zest of 1 orange
- 2 tablespoons honey or maple syrup
- 1 tablespoon balsamic vinegar
- 1/4 teaspoon ground cinnamon
- 1/4 teaspoon ground ginger
- Pinch of salt

For the Roasted Brussels Sprouts:

- 1 lb Brussels sprouts, trimmed and halved
- 1 tablespoon olive oil
- 1 teaspoon garlic powder
- Salt and pepper to taste
- 1/4 cup toasted walnuts or pecans (optional)
-

Steps :

1. Prepare the Cranberry-Orange Glaze:
   - In a small saucepan, combine the fresh cranberries, orange juice, orange zest, honey (or maple syrup), balsamic vinegar, cinnamon, ginger, and a pinch of salt.
   - Cook over medium heat, stirring occasionally, until the cranberries burst and the sauce thickens (about 8-10 minutes).
   - Once the glaze has thickened, remove it from the heat and set aside.

2. Roast the Brussels Sprouts:
   - Preheat the oven to 400°F (200°C).
   - Toss the halved Brussels sprouts with olive oil, garlic powder, salt, and pepper.
   - Spread them evenly on a baking sheet and roast for 20-25 minutes, shaking the pan halfway through for even roasting. If desired, add toasted walnuts or pecans in the last 5 minutes of roasting.

3. Bake the Salmon:
   - While the Brussels sprouts are roasting, prepare the salmon. Line a baking sheet with parchment paper or foil.
   - Rub the salmon fillets with olive oil and season with salt and pepper.
   - Place the fillets on the baking sheet, skin-side down, and bake in the oven for 12-15 minutes, or until the salmon is cooked through and flakes easily with a fork.

4. Glaze the Salmon:
   - During the last 5 minutes of baking, brush the cranberry-orange glaze generously over the salmon fillets.
   - Let the glaze caramelize slightly in the oven for an extra burst of flavor.

5. Serve:
   - Serve the glazed salmon alongside the roasted Brussels sprouts. Drizzle any extra cranberry-orange glaze over the top for added flavor.

YOGA OR STRETCHING

12 December

Hey Sister,
Today, we're going to show our bodies some extra love and care by moving in ways that feel good, soothing, and freeing. It's time to roll out your yoga mat or find a comfy spot on the floor for some gentle stretching. Whether you're a seasoned yogi or just starting out, today's focus is on releasing tension, finding your flow, and connecting with your body in a mindful, loving way.

Choose a quick yoga practice that fits your mood, whether it's a relaxing flow to help you decompress or a morning stretch to get your day started, or even some grounding postures to help you feel grounded. If you'd rather stretch, take your time and carefully go through your neck, shoulders, back, and hips, which are the places where you carry the greatest tension. There's no need to move quickly or exert excessive force. This is about moving in a way that feels loving and paying attention to your body.

Pay attention to your breath as you progress through your practice. Allow each breath to bring you peace and let each exhale let go of whatever tension or stress you may have been holding. Take note of how your body feels: how the stretches create space in your body, how your muscles loosen up, and how your thoughts start to calm down. Now is the time to put the day's cares behind you and just be in the moment.

Stretching and yoga are two very effective self-care techniques. They strengthen your body, increase flexibility, and relieve physical strain. **But in addition to their health benefits, these exercises are a great means of fostering a relationship with your inner self.** You may calm your thoughts, lessen tension, and develop a sense of balance and tranquility by concentrating on your breathing and movement. Particularly yoga has been demonstrated to lower anxiety, elevate mood, and even strengthen the immune system.

Contrarily, stretching is an easy yet powerful technique to improve range of motion, boost blood flow to your muscles, and guard against injury. **Frequent stretching can also aid with pain relief, posture correction, and energy restoration.** Stretching and yoga both promote awareness, which enables you to pay attention to your body's demands and remain in the present.

Give yourself permission to stretch, move, and take deep breaths today. Let this practice serve as a reminder that you deserve to feel good about your body, whether it takes the form of an entire yoga class or just a few minutes of stretching. Release any stress you may be carrying and accept the way your breath and movement are flowing. You should use this time to unplug, refuel, and get in touch with who you are.

13 December

LISTEN TO MUSIC

Hey Sister,
Today is all about letting the rhythm take over, lifting your spirits, and filling your soul with joy through the magic of music. Whether you're in the mood to relax, dance, or simply vibe with some good tunes, this day is dedicated to creating your own little soundtrack of happiness. So, let's dive into the music that makes your heart sing!

Make a playlist of your all-time favorite songs first; these should be the tunes that make you smile, the ones that remind you of wonderful times past, or the beats that make you want to dance. It might be a mash-up of your favorite songs, from uplifting jams that make you want to jump around your living room to soothing sounds that help you relax. Let this playlist represent you and the things that make you happy, no matter what your style may be.

When your playlist is prepared, choose a comfortable seat, close your eyes, and let the music carry you away. Alternatively, if dancing is what gets you going, turn up the music and dance as if no one else is around! As the melodies and rhythms engross you, allow the music to flow through you, releasing any tension or stress. This is your chance to let go, express yourself, and engage with the feelings that music so masterfully arouses.

Not only is music listening a great way to unwind, but it also has many incredible health advantages as a potent kind of self-care. **Research has demonstrated that listening to music can alleviate pain, anxiety, and stress. It can strengthen your immune system, elevate your mood, and generally make you feel better.** Your brain releases dopamine, a feel-good hormone, when you listen to music you enjoy, which can lift your spirits and help you unwind. In addition to taking you back to a different era or location, music may also help you see your goals and desires come true or evoke pleasant memories.

You will reap even greater rewards if you decide to dance along. Dancing is an excellent method to increase energy, strengthen your heart, and get your body moving. It's also a fantastic opportunity to let out your innermost feelings and express yourself. Dancing is also a pleasant, lively method to connect with oneself and may be a lot of fun.

So turn on the music today. **Let yourself to totally enjoy the moment, whether you're dancing, lounging, or just taking in the atmosphere.** Allow the beat to reawaken your inner delight and let the melodies and lyrics serve as a reminder of life's beauty.

14
December

ACT OF KINDNESS

Hey Sister,
Today, we're turning our hearts outward and embracing the beauty of kindness. It's a day to do something thoughtful for someone else, to spread a little extra love and warmth in a world that can always use more of it. The wonderful thing about kindness is that it doesn't have to be big or complicated—sometimes the simplest acts can make the biggest difference, both for the person on the receiving end and for you.

Consider a someone in your life who would benefit from a little encouragement today. Maybe it's a family member who consistently supports you, a friend you haven't spoken to in a while, or someone who has been going through a difficult moment. It might even be a complete stranger or someone you run into every day. **It doesn't matter how intricate your act of kindness is; what counts is the thoughtfulness that went into it.**

One way to start could be to write someone a sincere message expressing your appreciation for what they do and your thoughts for them. "Hey, just wanted to let you know you're on my mind and I'm so grateful to have you in my life," might be the simplest possible message. You might also send them a handmade card or message, which they may save and refer to anytime they need a reminder that they are loved. If you're in the mood for something crafty, you could make a batch of cookies to give to a neighbor or assemble a tiny care package for someone who might use a little extra attention.

There are many chances to show kindness today if you're out and about. Offer a sincere remark, hold the door open for someone, or simply listen intently to someone who needs to chat. **A mere grin has the capacity to make someone's day better; it's a tiny gesture that can have a big impact.** Additionally, remember to be kind to the people you come into contact with on a daily basis, such as your barista, the grocery store clerk, or the delivery person. Even small acts of kindness can make a huge difference in someone's life.

Kindness has the charm of spreading like wildfire. **Acts of kindness not only improve the other person's life but also lift your own spirits and encourage people to act kindly toward others.** This is supported by compelling science: doing good deeds causes our brains to release oxytocin, sometimes known as the "love hormone," which lowers blood pressure, reduces stress, and fosters emotions of contentment and connection. Additionally, practicing kindness causes the production of serotonin, a neurotransmitter that improves mood, fosters wellbeing, and even has therapeutic effects.

Studies have indicated that consistent acts of kindness might result in reduced anxiety and depressive symptoms, as well as a longer, healthier life. It's an easy, yet very effective, method to enhance your physical and emotional well-being. What's the best thing, then? Being kind is infectious. When you act kindly, it encourages others to follow suit, starting a domino effect of kindness and optimism.

So let's make it our goal to be kind today. Think for a moment about how you can add a little brightness, ease, or joy to someone else's day. And wherever you go throughout the day, seek for chances to show kindness to people, whether they be complete strangers, friends, or family. No matter how tiny, every act of kindness has the ability to change the world.

15 December

Hey Sister,
Today, let's carve out some time to pause, reflect, and take stock of our journeys so far. It's a day to look back on the goals and achievements that have shaped our year and to set meaningful intentions for the year ahead. This isn't just about ticking off boxes; it's about honoring your growth, celebrating your successes, and embracing the lessons that have come your way.

Locate a peaceful area where you can sit and reflect. You may even bring a cup of tea or coffee and your journal. **Consider the objectives you set for yourself at the start of the year**. Which dreams did you hope to pursue? What obstacles did you wish to get past? Whether or not you accomplished everything on your list, take a time to appreciate all of your hard work. Recall that progress is about all of your steps, no matter how big or small, taken along the path rather than just crossing the finish line.

Now consider the accomplishments of which you are most proud this year. Perhaps it was overcoming a fear, achieving a goal, or just a moment when you made a meaningful effort to take care of yourself. As you write things down, allow yourself to truly experience the pride and happiness of those times. Honor your victories because you merit it. You've made it through a challenging but rewarding year, and that's something to be proud of.

Spend some time thinking about the lessons you've learnt while you reflect. What difficulties did you encounter, and how did you overcome them? What self-awareness did you gain? These realizations are worth at least as much as your accomplishments. They serve as stepping stones to help you enter the new year with even greater power and insight.

It's time to look forward after taking stock of the past. **What goals would you like to achieve in the upcoming year? These don't have to be lofty goals; they might just be modest but important intents that are in line with your core beliefs.** Perhaps your goals are to develop your relationships, put more emphasis on self-care, or follow a joyful hobby. Let these intentions, whatever they may be, originate from a place of love and positivity rather than pressure or expectation.

Making plans is a great way to stay focused on the things that are really important to you. It's about making a plan that directs you toward living a purposeful and genuine life and coordinating your activities with your principles. This is supported by some excellent evidence, which demonstrates that establishing precise, **well-defined goals can boost performance, motivate individuals, and enhance wellbeing.** Thinking back on your objectives and successes gives you the chance to congratulate yourself on your advancements and boost your self-esteem, both of which can motivate you to keep going.

Thus, use this opportunity to think back on your adventure today. Respect the objectives you've worked toward, acknowledge your successes, and learn from your mistakes. And remember that you have the fortitude, resiliency, and discernment to build the life you desire as you make your intentions for the coming year with an open heart.

My New Year
Goals

1.

2.

3.

4.

16 December

Hey Sister,
Today, we're embracing a practice that's all about finding deeper connection—by disconnecting. It's time to unplug from the endless notifications, screens, and digital noise, and instead, focus on the connections that truly matter. Whether it's spending quality time with loved ones or reconnecting with yourself, today is all about being fully present in the moment.

To begin, switch off your phone, log out of social media, and put away any other gadgets that have a tendency to take up your time. **We're so used to being connected all the time that I know it may feel a little weird at first, but I promise that this digital detox will feel like a breath of fresh air.**

Make the most of your time with loved ones if you are spending it with them today. Without the distraction of electronics, engage in meaningful conversation, play a game, prepare a meal together, or simply spend time together. When we're really present with the people we care about, these moments of connection are what really strengthen our bonds and produce enduring memories.

Use this time to re-establish a connection with what makes you happy and peaceful if you have the day to yourself. Perhaps you'll meditate, go for a stroll in the park, curl up with a good book, or just take in the silence. This is your time to ponder, listen to your own ideas, and give yourself permission to simply be. **One of the most effective types of self-care is reconnecting with oneself, which frequently results in increased inner calm, creativity, and clarity.**

The benefits of unplugging from technology are backed by some strong science. We can become more stressed, have shorter attention spans, and even have sleep disturbances if we are constantly surrounded by screens and digital media. **By regularly disconnecting from technology, we give our minds a chance to recuperate. This enhances our general wellbeing, sharpens our focus, and lowers stress levels.** Research has also demonstrated that spending time offline, particularly with those we love, can build bonds and elevate our mood by encouraging richer, more meaningful interactions.

Give yourself permission to disconnect from the digital world today. Pay attention to what's in front of you, such as the people you love, the scenery, and the ideas and emotions that come up when you give yourself permission to be present. Reconnecting with what really matters and removing yourself from the incessant noise may surprise you with how refreshing it feels.

17 December

SKIN CARE RITUAL

Hey Beautiful,
Today, we're treating ourselves to a little extra love and care with a soothing skincare ritual. It's all about taking the time to focus on your skin, giving it the attention it deserves, and embracing the joy that comes from nurturing yourself. Whether it's exfoliating, moisturizing, or giving yourself a gentle facial massage, this is your moment to indulge in some well-deserved self-care.

Consider first what your skin needs right now. Perhaps a thorough cleansing followed by a mild exfoliation is necessary to get rid of any dead skin cells and show the healthy glow underneath. Alternatively, it might be a really moisturizing and softening product that leaves your skin feeling nourished and luminous. Try a facial massage if you're in the mood for something particularly special. Use your preferred oil or serum and gently massage your face in circular strokes, paying specific attention to the forehead, temples, and jawline—areas where you carry stress. This promotes a healthy, natural glow and increases circulation in addition to feeling fantastic.

Pay attention to the feelings you experience during your skincare routine, such as the softness of the products, the comforting touch of your hands, and the relaxing aromas in the air. **Embrace this moment to the fullest, feeling grateful for your skin's care and the way it makes you feel.** Knowing that you're doing something positive for your skin and spirit when you're taking the time to take care of yourself in this way is immensely powerful.

The best thing is that skincare is about feeling well as well as looking beautiful. **According to science, taking good care of your skin might improve your general health. By encouraging attention and relaxation, the straightforward actions of washing, moisturizing, or massaging your skin can help lower tension and anxiety.** Your parasympathetic nervous system, which aids in relaxation, is triggered when you concentrate on the calming, repetitive movements of your skincare routine. Furthermore, having well-maintained, healthy skin can increase your self-esteem and sense of comfort in your own skin, both literally and figuratively.

Skincare routines are another lovely method to cultivate self-love. You are telling yourself that you are deserving of kindness, attention, and care when you take the time to take care of your skin. It's a simple yet effective method to honor your body, love yourself, and discover your inner beauty.

Thus, let's embrace skincare rituals as a type of self-care today. Take this time to treat yourself and enjoy the process, whether it's a brief routine or an opulent session. **Both your skin and your spirit will appreciate it.**

18 December

MEDITATION

Hey Sister,
Today, we're diving into the beautiful practice of meditation—a moment to pause, breathe, and find stillness in the midst of all that life throws our way. It's a day to dedicate some time just for you, to tune into your inner self, and to let go of whatever's weighing on your mind. Whether you're new to meditation or it's something you've done before, today is all about reconnecting with your breath, your thoughts, and the peaceful space within you.

Don't worry if you don't know where to begin; **meditation doesn't have to be difficult**. All you have to do is locate a peaceful, comfortable area, close your eyes, and concentrate on your breathing. Breathe in deeply, allowing the air to fill your lungs, and then slowly release the air, releasing any tension or stress. When you breathe, attempt to rid your mind of any distractions and return your attention to your breath whenever your mind wanders. Your thoughts will naturally wander; that's all part of the process. Simply return to your breathing and the rhythm that grounds you with gentle guidance.

There are several of guided meditations available to aid you through the practice if you would want a bit more direction. **Guiding meditations can be a great method to explore various facets of meditation and enhance your practice, regardless of your individual goals, such as self-compassion, gratitude, or relaxation.**

Because it enables you to develop a sense of peace and clarity in the middle of the craziness of everyday life, meditation is an incredibly effective kind of self-care. **You are giving yourself the gift of presence when you dedicate a short period of time to meditation.** This practice allows you to decelerate, inhale deeply, and establish a connection with your inner tranquility. It's as if you've pressed the mental reset button, giving you the clarity and composure to tackle the remainder of your day.

The health advantages of meditation are also well supported by science. **Frequent meditation has been demonstrated to lower blood pressure, lessen stress, and enhance concentration and focus.** It can strengthen your immune system, enhance sleep, and lessen anxiety and despair. Meditation functions by establishing a state of balance and relaxation, reducing cortisol levels (the stress hormone), and relaxing the neurological system. With time, it can also aid in the development of stronger emotional resilience, which will make it easier and more graceful for you to deal with life's obstacles.

So let's use this opportunity to meditate together today. Allow yourself to totally commit to this practice, whether it lasts for five or fifty minutes. **Take a deep breath, release the things you don't need, and rediscover the calm, strong person you are.** Remind yourself that this is the moment to refuel, center, and regain equilibrium.

19
December

JOURNAL YOUR THOUGHTS

Hey Sister,
Today, we're opening up a space just for you—a place where you can let your thoughts flow freely, where your feelings can find their voice, and where you can simply be. It's time to grab your journal, a pen, and maybe a cozy spot where you feel comfortable and at ease. Today is all about journaling your thoughts, releasing whatever's on your mind, and giving yourself the gift of self-expression.

This can be done in any way you like. Writing in a journal is an extremely personal activity that revolves around your own desires. Perhaps you should start by writing about your day, including any noteworthy encounters, thoughts, or feelings. Alternatively, you might like to delve farther, investigating feelings that have been brewing beneath the surface, aspirations you've been fostering, or difficulties you're encountering. **Allow the words to flow freely, without hesitation or judgment. You can be genuine, unvarnished, and honest with yourself in this environment.**

It's also acceptable if you're not sure where to start. Starting with a straightforward question like "Today, I feel..." or "Lately, I've been thinking about..." can occasionally help open the floodgates. Let your pen glide over the page as your thoughts flow, without worrying about grammar, spelling, or perfection. Additionally, if you find yourself stopping, give yourself the room and time you need to consider your options. This is a place of freedom to express oneself without pressure or hurry.

Because it provides a safe, judgment-free environment for you to process your ideas and feelings, journaling is an effective kind of self-care. **It's similar to having a talk with oneself, where you can ruminate on your past, examine your deepest emotions, and learn more about your own heart and mind.** Writing things down can also assist you in organizing your ideas, resolving conflicting feelings, and even gaining previously unconsidered fresh insights.

Additionally, the advantages of journaling are supported by some amazing evidence. **Writing about your ideas and feelings on a regular basis has been found to lower stress, elevate mood, and enhance brain clarity.** Because it offers a positive outlet for addressing feelings and difficulties, journaling can also help you become more emotionally resilient. It has been connected to better problem-solving skills and may even raise your general wellbeing. Additionally, journaling helps you practice mindfulness, which is being in the present moment with your thoughts and feelings. This can help you become more self-aware and evolve as a person.

So let's write everything that's on our thoughts on those pages today. Allow your journal to be a reflection of your current state of mind, identity, and location. This is your opportunity to delve further into self-exploration, self-expression, and deeper self-connection—whether you write a few words or several pages.

20
December

SELF-COMPASSION

Hey Sister,
Today, we're turning our hearts inward with a practice that's so important but often overlooked —self-compassion. It's about being gentle with yourself, acknowledging your struggles, and offering yourself the same kindness and understanding that you would so freely give to a dear friend. Let's take this day to really embrace the idea of being our own best friend, and to treat ourselves with the love and care we deserve.

To begin, pause to consider something that has been causing you difficulty recently. It could be anything, such as a problem at work, a challenging relationship, or even an error you've committed that has been bothering you. **Allow yourself the time and space to properly accept whatever it is. It's acceptable to feel the way you do. We've all had moments when we feel unworthy or fumble through life's challenges.**

Imagine now that a close friend confided in you about experiencing a similar struggle. **In what way would you reply to them?** It's likely that you would console them, tell them that they're doing their hardest, and tell them it's alright if they don't have everything worked out. You would demonstrate compassion, empathy, and love for them. I want you to speak to yourself with the same kindness and words today.

Have gentle words with yourself. In case you've been harsh with yourself, inhale deeply and release that negativity. Consider how far you've gone, how much you've experienced, and the strength it has required to get to this point rather than what you believe you have done wrong. **Remind yourself that struggles are normal.** Since I'm only human, I'm trying my hardest. Permit oneself to be human, to make errors, and to use those lessons to improve.

Self-compassion is acknowledging that everyone suffers difficulties and that you should be treated with the same tolerance and kindness that you show others. It is not about running from responsibilities or coming up with excuses. **By engaging in self-compassionate practices, you're fostering resilience and your mental health.** Having compassion for yourself makes you more resilient to life's challenges and more capable of overcoming failures.

The science is unambiguous: practicing self-compassion has numerous advantages. **Studies indicate that those who engage in self-compassion practices typically experience reduced levels of anxiety and sadness, enhanced emotional control, and an overall increase in well-being.** Additionally, self-compassion fosters a more positive and balanced way of thinking, lessening the negative consequences of self-criticism and enabling you to face obstacles head-on. A deeper sense of self-worth, resilience, and motivation can all result from this exercise.

So let us treat ourselves gently today. Recognize your difficulties, but try not to let them define who you are. Rather, be kind and understanding to yourself as you deserve. Never forget that you are doing your absolute best, and that is sufficient. You are sufficient.

21 December

Hey Sister,
Today, we're slowing down to savor one of life's simplest and most comforting pleasures—a warm, delicious drink. Whether it's a cup of tea, coffee, hot cocoa, or any other beverage that makes you feel cozy and content, this is your moment to pause, breathe, and truly enjoy every sip. Let's make this day all about finding comfort and joy in the little things.

Make your preferred hot beverage first. Take your time; steep your coffee to your preferred strength, make a rich, creamy cup of hot cocoa, or select tea leaves that bring you joy. Perhaps you'll top it with a sprinkling of something unique, a dollop of cream, or a dash of cinnamon. **Make the most of this moment by living it to the fullest.**

When your drink is ready, locate a quiet area to sit and unwind. Breathe deeply as you round the mug with your hands, allowing the warmth to sink into your fingers. **Allow the taste to saturate your senses as you take your first drink.** As you swallow, take note of the flavor, the temperature, and the sensation. Allow yourself to enjoy the small pleasures of a warm drink on a chilly day, and allow yourself to be completely present in this moment.

Try not to get distracted while you enjoy each drink. This is your moment to relax, take in the silence, and just be. For a brief period, you could even close your eyes and allow the warmth of the beverage and the tranquility of the surroundings to envelope you. **This is more than just sipping your favorite beverage; it's about establishing a little mindfulness ritual that gives you a chance to unwind and reconnect with yourself during a hectic day.**

Here's why this little habit has such immense power: consciously enjoying a hot beverage can have some amazing advantages for your health. It's easier to de-stress and encourage relaxation when you take the time to slow down and truly experience your senses. Concentrating on the here and now can ease anxiety, quiet the mind, and provide a sense of contentment and serenity. Additionally, this exercise promotes mindfulness, which has been demonstrated to increase general happiness, improve mental clarity, and enhance emotional regulation.

You're also giving yourself a vacation from the hectic pace of everyday life by taking your time sipping your drink. It's a time to take a deep breath, refuel, and remind yourself that it's acceptable to give the simple things in life some more time. Your energy and mood can be greatly affected by these brief mindfulness exercises, which can make you feel more balanced and in control of your life.

Let's enjoy this time together while sipping our hot beverages today. Let every drink serve as a gentle reminder that you deserve to take it easy, to savor the tiny things in life, and to take small but meaningful care of yourself.

SPICED ORANGE HOT CHOCOLATE

This twist on classic hot chocolate combines rich cocoa with the bright, zesty flavor of oranges and a hint of warm spices. Perfect for cozying up by the fire!

Ingredients:

- 2 cups milk (dairy or plant-based)
- 1/4 cup cocoa powder
- 1/4 cup dark chocolate chips
- 2 tablespoons sugar or honey
- Zest of 1 orange
- 1/2 teaspoon cinnamon
- 1/4 teaspoon nutmeg
- Whipped cream (optional)
- Orange slices or zest for garnish

Instructions:

1. In a saucepan, heat the milk over medium heat until warm but not boiling.
2. Whisk in the cocoa powder, chocolate chips, sugar, orange zest, cinnamon, and nutmeg until smooth and fully combined.
3. Continue stirring over low heat until the chocolate is melted and the mixture is steaming.
4. Pour into a mug, top with whipped cream (if desired), and garnish with an orange slice or extra zest.
5. Sip slowly and enjoy the combination of rich chocolate and bright cit.

**22
December**

MOVIE NIGHT

**Hey Sister,
Today, we're indulging in one of the coziest and most joyful forms of self-care—a movie night! It's time to pick a film that uplifts your spirits, makes you smile, or simply brings you that warm, fuzzy feeling inside. Let's create a little oasis of comfort and joy, where you can relax, unwind, and let the magic of the movies take you away.**

Select a movie that resonates with you first. Maybe it's a feel-good movie you've been longing to see, or maybe it's your all-time favorite that you've watched a hundred times and never grow weary of. **The secret is to choose something that uplifts and makes you joyful, whether it's an animated classic, a sentimental drama, or a romantic comedy.**

It's time to arrange the stage after you have your movie in mind. Fluff up your cushions, grab your softest blanket, and turn down the lights to create the coziest setting imaginable. To give a little more radiance, consider lighting a few candles or plugging in some fairy lights. Remember to bring snacks! Pour a hot beverage, pop some popcorn, or indulge in something sweet for yourself. Make this your night, however comfortable and enjoyable you like.

Allow yourself to unwind completely as you settle in to watch your movie. **Cuddle up under your blanket and sink into the cushions while the movie takes you to a different realm.** As you fully immerse yourself in the experience, let the story unfold, laugh aloud, and cry if necessary. This is your chance to unwind, feel good, and savor the pure delight of a fantastic film.

But this habit isn't simply for amusement; movie evenings are a great method to elevate your emotions and reduce stress. Dopamine is a neurotransmitter that elevates mood and produces pleasurable feelings. It might be released when you watch a movie you adore. **Videos that inspire or make you laugh might also help you feel less stressed and anxious by taking your mind off of your daily concerns.** Furthermore, movies have a way of re-establishing a connection between us and our emotions, enabling us to analyze emotions, see the world from fresh angles, and even find solace in watching our own experiences portrayed on screen.

For your movie night, setting up a pleasant environment provides even more coziness and ease. A feeling of routine and intentionality can be created by carefully arranging your area, such as selecting your favorite blanket and making your favorite snacks. This improves the experience and lets your body and mind know when it's time to relax and get some much-needed sleep.

So let's enjoy the pleasure of a movie night this evening. Choose a happy movie, curl up, and give yourself permission to enjoy this moment to the fullest. **Allow yourself to be happy for a minute, no matter if you're watching by yourself or with loved ones.**

Here's a list of heartwarming, feel-good movies perfect for a cozy self-care movie night, guaranteed to uplift your spirits and bring that warm, fuzzy feeling inside

1. The Holiday (2006)
A perfect Christmas-themed romantic comedy that follows two women, both dealing with relationship struggles, as they swap homes for the holidays and discover love in unexpected places. This film is light, fun, and heartwarming.

2. Pride and Prejudice (2005)
A beautiful adaptation of Jane Austen's classic novel, full of romance, wit, and breathtaking scenery. The story of Elizabeth Bennet and Mr. Darcy will fill you with warmth and inspiration.

3. Julie & Julia (2009)
A delightful film about cooking, self-discovery, and perseverance, as it interweaves the stories of Julia Child and a modern-day blogger who takes on the challenge of cooking all of Julia's recipes. It's perfect for food lovers and those needing a little inspiration to pursue their passions.

4. Little Women (2019)
This modern adaptation of Louisa May Alcott's classic novel is a celebration of sisterhood, creativity, and the strength of women. With beautiful cinematography and touching performances, it's a heartwarming and empowering film.

5. La La Land (2016)
A visually stunning and musical journey about chasing dreams and finding love in Los Angeles. It's a film that will make you smile, laugh, and possibly cry, but leaves you feeling inspired.

6. Mamma Mia! (2008)
A fun, feel-good musical filled with ABBA's greatest hits, vibrant performances, and sun-drenched island vibes. It's impossible not to sing along and feel a wave of happiness while watching this film.

23
December

AROMATIC BATH

Hey Sister,
Today, we're embracing the ultimate form of relaxation—an aromatic bath. It's time to draw yourself a warm, soothing bath and let all the stress and tension of the day melt away. Whether you're using Epsom salts, essential oils, or a fizzy bath bomb, this is your time to unwind, pamper yourself, and soak in some well-deserved tranquility.

Prepare the space for your bath beforehand. Maybe turn down the lights, light a few candles, and turn on some relaxing music. Pick the ingredients that speak to you right now. Perhaps it's a colorful bath bomb to add a little extra excitement to your soak, a few drops of your favorite essential oil to create a peaceful atmosphere, or Epsom salts to ease sore muscles. **Consider this small act of self-care while the water fills the tub, knowing that you are going to give yourself the wonderful gift of relaxation.**

Let your body unwind completely as you submerge itself in the warm water. As the relaxing aromas of the oils or salts fill your senses, feel the tightness in your muscles begin to dissipate. Shut your eyes, inhale deeply, and give yourself permission to be fully present at this instant. This is your time to relax, forget about the stresses of the day, and just take in the comforting warmth of the bathtub.

You can indulge a little more during your bath time if you'd like. You could read a good book, drink herbal tea, or just take in the silence. **Choose whatever works best for you, but make sure your entire attention is on unwinding and taking care of yourself.**

Taking an aromatic bath has several advantages beyond making you feel wonderful right away. For example, epsom salts are well-known for their capacity to ease pain in the muscles, lessen inflammation, and aid in the body's detoxification process. Additionally helping to improve sleep and lessen stress is the magnesium found in Epsom salts. The therapeutic benefits of essential oils, such as lavender, eucalyptus, and chamomile, range from mind-calming to respiratory problems relief to skin-soothing. **The warm water itself has the potential to enhance circulation, reduce joint discomfort, and encourage relaxation, leaving you feeling more invigorated and renewed.**

Taking a bath with these additional elements also stimulates your senses, which helps improve awareness and help you focus entirely on the here and now. This small act of making time for yourself conveys to your body and mind that you are deserving of this kind of attention and care. It's a lovely kind of self-care that supports self-reset, self-recharge, and self-reconnection.

So let's turn our bath time into a real haven this evening. Savor every moment of the warmth, aromas, and tranquility that it brings. Sister, you deserve to unwind for a while. Use this time to practice self-care and tranquility.

24 December

Hey Sister,

We've reached the final day of our self-care journey, and what a beautiful journey it's been! Today is a day for reflection and celebration—a time to look back on the past 23 days and honor every bit of love, care, and kindness you've shown yourself this month. You've made a powerful commitment to nurture your mind, body, and soul, and today, let's take a moment to truly appreciate all that you've done.

Look for a nice, peaceful place to sit that is comfortable. Perhaps pour yourself a nice beverage, light a candle, and cover yourself with a cozy blanket. Breathe deeply for a few moments, and as you release the air, let your mind to wander back over the previous several weeks. **Consider all of the self-care rituals you have adopted, such as enjoying a warm beverage, having a fragrant bath, writing in a notebook, engaging in self-compassion exercises, or just pausing to breathe and be in the moment.**

Consider your feelings while you consider these practices. How have they aided in your self-reconnection? What fresh perspectives have you acquired? In what ways, even the tiniest ones, have you grown? This journey has been more than just isolated self-care sessions; it has involved developing a closer bond with yourself, learning to pay attention to your needs, and realizing your value.

Now let's honor all of your accomplishments, both large and small. You may have experienced days when self-care was simple for you and days when it was more difficult. Both merit celebration on an equal footing. Maybe you developed a stronger feeling of awareness, learned new techniques for unwinding, or enjoyed being creative. Alternatively, it's possible that you merely granted yourself permission to relax and rejuvenate, realizing that this is also an effective kind of self-care. Whatever your path was, pause to pay tribute to it. It's so lovely that you've showed yourself love.

This is not the conclusion of the self-care journey. **You can use the habits you've adopted over the course of these 24 days as tools well into the upcoming year.** They serve as a reminder that practicing self-care is a continuous rather than an isolated activity. It's a commitment to continue taking care of your body, mind, and soul, to put your health first, and to continue loving and caring for yourself in the same way that you do for other people.

Not only is it a therapeutic activity, but thinking back on and acknowledging your journey toward self-care is also very healthy for your overall health. Research indicates that consistent self-care practices can lower stress, enhance mental well-being, and raise emotions of contentment and enjoyment. **By giving yourself the time and attention you deserve, you've bolstered your resilience, developed a closer bond with yourself, and established the groundwork for a happier, more mindful existence in addition to supporting your physical and mental well-being.**

So let's rejoice today! Honor your dedication to yourself, your accomplishments, and the self-love you've demonstrated. You have accomplished something genuinely amazing for yourself, so celebrate it anyway you choose—by treating yourself to a nice treat, having a private moment of appreciation, or just realizing how strong and mature you have become.

HERE'S A LIST OF SCIENTIFIC STUDIES AND RESEARCH SUPPORTING THE BENEFITS OF THE SELF-CARE PRACTICES MENTIONED IN THIS SELF-CARE ADVENT CALENDAR

1. Gratitude Journaling
   - Research: Studies show that regularly practicing gratitude can improve mental health, enhance well-being, and increase happiness.
   - Source: A study published in Personality and Individual Differences found that people who regularly express gratitude experience more positive emotions and greater life satisfaction (Wood et al., 2010).

2. Pampering Yourself (Spa Day)
   - Research: Relaxation techniques such as bathing or skincare routines reduce stress and improve mood.
   - Source: A study in Complementary Therapies in Clinical Practice showed that aromatherapy and self-care routines can lower stress levels and improve mood (Lee, 2011).

3. Digital Detox
   - Research: Reducing screen time and unplugging from digital devices has been shown to lower stress, improve sleep, and enhance focus.
   - Source: A study in Journal of Behavioral Addictions highlights how digital detoxing improves psychological well-being and lowers stress (Przybylski & Weinstein, 2017).

4. Mindful Breathing
   - Research: Deep, mindful breathing exercises activate the parasympathetic nervous system, which reduces stress and promotes relaxation.
   - Source: A study in Frontiers in Psychology shows that deep breathing improves mood, reduces anxiety, and can have positive effects on overall health (Zaccaro et al., 2018).

5. Aromatherapy
   - Research: Aromatherapy has been found to reduce stress, anxiety, and improve sleep quality.
   - Source: A study published in The Journal of Alternative and Complementary Medicine found that essential oils, such as lavender, have a calming effect and reduce stress and anxiety (Conrad & Adams, 2012).

6. Nature Walk
- Research: Spending time in nature, often referred to as "forest bathing," has been shown to lower blood pressure, reduce cortisol levels, and enhance mood.
- Source: A study in Environmental Health and Preventive Medicine demonstrated that spending time in nature can reduce stress and improve mental health (Li, 2010).

7. Hydration Reminder
- Research: Proper hydration boosts energy levels, improves cognitive function, and promotes a positive mood.
- Source: Research published in The Journal of Nutrition shows that mild dehydration negatively affects mood and cognitive performance (Armstrong et al., 2012).

8. Indulge in a Good Book
- Research: Reading for just six minutes a day can reduce stress by 68%, lower heart rate, and improve relaxation.
- Source: A study from the University of Sussex found that reading can reduce stress and increase relaxation more than listening to music or taking a walk (Lewis, 2009).

9. Affirmations
- Research: Practicing positive affirmations activates the brain's reward system and helps improve self-esteem and reduce negative thoughts.
- Source: A study in Social Cognitive and Affective Neuroscience shows that self-affirmations activate brain regions associated with reward and positive valuation (Cascio et al., 2016).

10. Creative Expression
- Research: Engaging in creative activities like drawing or painting reduces stress, improves mood, and can serve as a therapeutic outlet.
- Source: A study in The Arts in Psychotherapy found that engaging in art-making significantly reduces stress hormone levels (Kaimal et al., 2016).

11. Healthy Meal
- Research: Eating nutrient-rich foods has been linked to better mental health, increased energy, and improved mood.
- Source: A study published in The Lancet Psychiatry shows that a balanced, healthy diet is associated with reduced risks of depression and improved mental health (Jacka et al., 2017).

12. Yoga or Stretching
- Research: Regular yoga or stretching helps release muscle tension, reduce anxiety, and improve emotional regulation.
- Source: A study in Frontiers in Psychiatry reveals that yoga can reduce stress, improve emotional balance, and enhance overall mental well-being (Balasubramaniam et al., 2013).

13. Listening to Music
- Research: Listening to music triggers the release of dopamine, improving mood and reducing stress.
- Source: A study published in Nature Neuroscience found that music activates the brain's reward system, promoting feelings of pleasure (Salimpoor et al., 2013).

14. Acts of Kindness
- Research: Performing acts of kindness increases happiness, reduces stress, and fosters emotional well-being.
- Source: Research in Emotion journal found that acts of kindness enhance well-being, reduce stress, and improve overall emotional health (Aknin et al., 2013).

15. Goal Reflection
- Research: Reflecting on past goals and achievements promotes self-awareness and helps set future intentions, improving motivation and emotional well-being.
- Source: Studies in Psychological Science show that reflecting on personal growth can increase happiness and motivation (Emmons & McCullough, 2003).

16. Disconnect for Reconnection
- Research: Disconnecting from technology and spending time with loved ones or alone can improve focus, deepen relationships, and reduce stress.
- Source: A study in The Journal of Social and Personal Relationships revealed that disconnecting from digital devices can improve relationship quality and emotional well-being (Roberts & David, 2016).

17. Skincare Ritual
- Research: Engaging in skincare routines reduces stress, enhances self-esteem, and promotes mindfulness.
- Source: Studies in Complementary Therapies in Medicine show that skincare rituals help activate the parasympathetic nervous system, which calms the body and mind (Perry & Becerra, 2017).

18. Meditation
   - Research: Meditation is known to reduce stress, improve concentration, and promote emotional health.
   - Source: A study in JAMA Internal Medicine found that mindfulness meditation helps reduce stress and improve overall well-being (Goyal et al., 2014).
19. Journaling
   - Research: Writing about thoughts and emotions helps reduce stress, improve mental clarity, and enhance emotional well-being.
   - Source: Research published in Advances in Psychiatric Treatment shows that expressive writing improves mood, reduces stress, and supports emotional processing (Baikie & Wilhelm, 2005).
20. Self-Compassion
   - Research: Practicing self-compassion leads to lower levels of stress, anxiety, and depression, while fostering emotional resilience.
   - Source: A study in Clinical Psychology Review showed that self-compassion helps regulate emotions and improve psychological health (Neff, 2003).
21. Savoring a Hot Beverage.
   - Source: Research in Psychological Science found that savoring simple experiences, like drinking a warm beverage, enhances positive emotions and life satisfaction (Bryant & Veroff, 2007).
22. Movie Night
   - Research: Watching movies, particularly uplifting or nostalgic films, can improve mood and decrease stress.
   - Source: A study published in Cognitive Research: Principles and Implications found that watching movies helps regulate emotions, decrease stress, and foster relaxation (Gregory et al., 2020).
23. Aromatic Bath
   - Research: Taking baths with Epsom salts and essential oils promotes relaxation, relieves muscle tension, and improves mood.
   - Source: A study published in Evidence-Based Complementary and Alternative Medicine found that warm baths, especially with aromatherapy, reduce stress and improve physical well-being (Watanabe et al., 2020).
24. Reflect and Celebrate
   - Source: Studies in Journal of Personality and Social Psychology show that reflecting on achievements promotes well-being, happiness, and sustained motivation (Sheldon & Lyubomirsky, 2006).

NOTES

Made in United States
Troutdale, OR
11/07/2024

24550705R00046